acknowledge our benevolent presence in USA border and should recommend us for "Noble Peace Prize" collectively.

What is the root cause of "so called terrorism"?

Someone says, "Pakistanis hate Americans so much that they are ready to risk their lives to infiltrate to USA and kill Americans". Someone else says, "Killing Kafir is religious duty of Pakistanis". Someone else says, "In Pakistan there is severe unemployment issue, in lieu of starving to death, if a Pakistani gets 200 USD cash. He is ready to strap a suicide vest and come to USA. Are these real reasons of war between USA and Pakistan? Or do we need to dig deep down to the problem of terrorists?

Think for a moment, if you are having good food, good wine and good sex on a daily basis, would you be ready to put a suicide vest under your chest, take up arms against the formidable USA Army and get yourself killed?

What is missing in terrorist's life? This picture depicts a letter written by a terrorist to his family.

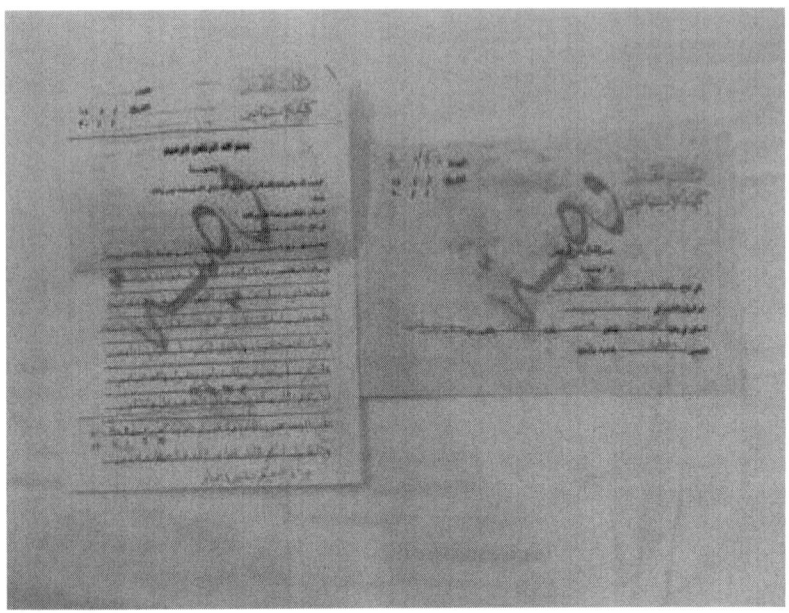

The letter says,

Dear Parent,

Do not be sad for my death, do not wear black clothes to mourn my death.

I asked you to get myself married, you said, "I do not earn enough to support family, I should not marry".

Now I am going to marry 72 virgin by God's grace.

Your Son

Fatwa: Hunted in America

This book is dedicated to all Americans.

Disclaimer: All characters, companies, events, places mentioned in the book are purely fictitious, any similarity with a person or company or event or place is purely coincidental.

Introduction

I am Pamela, a research student at UCLA. My uncle was in Army, he was killed by Pakistani terrorists. My uncle's death still pains me a lot. It left an incurable scar on my soul.

But I do not believe that Pakistan killed my uncle, I believe that war killed my uncle. I have done extensive research on the problem of terrorism, war between USA and Pakistan. By almighty's grace, I have come up with a viable solution to end war between USA and Pakistan forever, which would also end the problem of "so called terrorism" once and for all. We have tried and tested the solution in border of USA and infiltration has reduced significantly by using our idea. I also take the opportunity to thank Mark Zuckerberg for coming up with Facebook platform. We have used Facebook extensively to solve terrorist's problem. UN must

Solution to the problem of terrorism

This letter struck me like lightening. I started running in the street yelling. "Eureka, Eureka, I have found the root cause of terrorism".

It's not poverty, it's not hatred between USA and Pakistan. Just because terrorists are deprived of good sex, they are ready to martyr themselves and go to the utopian world where they are supposed to get 72 virgins to satisfy their sex needs!

I called upon all of my "Married But Available" female friends and hatched upon a plan.

As readers may already be aware that now many married girls are sleeping with dozens of people (be it boss, be it driver, be it friend, be it casual contact, be it lunch date, be it dinner date, be it security guard, etc.). Thanks to "Family Planning Pills" and Facebook! Terrorists are coming from Pakistan to get killed by USA Army so that they can get 72 virgins after death. Why do not we have sex with any terrorist who infiltrates USA and send them back to Pakistan sexually satisfied?

To test our Idea, We started a Facebook private group named, "Married But Available".

My friend Roseme was tasked to sign up new members. Most women had accumulated lot of guilty feelings as in some corner of their heart, they felt, "Sleeping with other males after marriage is sinful"

To clean the accumulated sins, we gave them the idea to serve at USA border. Roseme blackmailed "Married But Available" girls emotionally saying, "See just because a Pakistani terrorist is poor, just because, he cannot take you out for a lunch/dinner, just because he cannot give you costly gift, you are not ready to sleep with him? This is gross injustice, almighty will not forgive your sins and you will burn in hell forever."

Someone refuted Roseme, saying that, "It's my body, I can decide whom to give and whom to not give. Also terrorist from Pakistans are dirty, they do not take bath and they may be carrying STD, what happens to our body after having sex with Pakistani Terrorists?"

I assured them, "We will make all Pakistani terrorists take bath and wear condom before touching any of us."

Another lady complained, "What if they come in group and rape us?"

Roseme replied immediately, "We will only allow one terrorist at a time, if we are unable to handle him, we will forcefully evict him from our camp"

We were group of 20 women coming from different parts of America. We setup a camp on top of a hill close to "Mississippi River" near USA border. We put following advertisement in all four side of the camps.

DEAR JIHADIS, WE ARE 20 SEXY GIRLS STAYING IN

THE CAMP, COME AND HAVE SEX WITH US FOR FREE!

DO NOT DIE IN THE HAND OF FORMIDABLE USA

MILITARY FOR 72 VIRGINS

HAVE YOU NOT HEARD THE PROVERB THAT, "ONE

BIRD IN HAND IS WORTH MORE THAN 2 BIRDS IN

BUSH?"

PLEASE GIVE OUR "MARRIED BUT AVAILABLE" GROUP

A TRY, YOU WILL NOT REPENT. GIVE US ONE CHANCE

TO SERVE YOU BEFORE GETTING YOURSELF KILLED IN

THE HAND OF FORMIDABLE AMERICAN ARMY.

We started waiting patiently for Pakistani terrorists to infiltrate border and have sex with us. First night was very cold, many of the girls in our group were dreaming of "warm love making".

It was 7 PM, we had our dinner, cold breeze was blowing and the moon light was unforgivingly shining on 20 patriotic women. The moon did not seem to give a damn about our noble initiative to come to USA border to solve the problem of "so called terrorism" between USA and Pakistan forever.

Suddenly five Pakistani terrorists barged into out camp and pointed their AK 47 towards us and yelled, "We have come to have sex, take off your clothes before we tear it off!"

All of the girls were shivering in fear of rape, they were also equally excited to serve Pakistani terrorists as a token of patriotism.

Roseme gathered some courage and yelled at terrorists, "No rape please, we want consensual sex only, if you want to rape us, we will yell, Allah hu Akbar, Pakistan Zindabad and burst small chocolate crackers, American Army can locate the target from noise, they will bomb our camp immediately.

The terrorists got confused, "Why to die even before having sex?"

The terrorist manager said, "OK, we will not rape you, tell us, what we need to do to have sex with all twenty girls?"

Roseme said, "First condition is, only one guy will be allowed at a time, he has to take bath in the Missisipi river, we will supply free soap and shampoo. We will make him wear condom before any girl will allow him to touch her. Is that a deal?"

The five Pakistani terrorists discussed among themselves and decided to agree on our condition. All of them stored their arms and ammunitions in our camp and went to take bath in the river hurriedly.

First terrorist came running to our camp within 10 minutes, he was wearing a Bermuda with his huge erected dick. He was shivering in excitement and yelled, "I am ready for sex. I am going to fuck all of you!"

He again yelled, "Who is first?"

Roseme volunteered to be the first sex patriot. The terrorist grabbed Roseme like a bear, kissed her, pressed her boob, put his hand inside Roseme's skirt. Then he made Roseme lie down on the camp bed and started rubbing his erect dick under Roseme's skirt. Roseme was enjoying it, she was breathing heavily. Roseme slapped the terrorist hard as terrorist was trying to take her innerwear out, she then handed over a condom, the terrorist wore it quickly and went inside Roseme with full force, Roseme moaned little bit and then just after two minutes, the terrorist ejaculated, he lost his erection completely and tried to get up from Roseme's body. Roseme was aroused, she was not ready to let the terrorist go and yelled, "I have satisfied you, now you have to satisfy myself in return!" The terrorist pleaded with folded hand, "I already lost my erection and please let me go!" Roseme yelled, "Use your tongue then, I will not let you go, till I orgasm, the terrorist used his tongue into Roseme's and after half an hour, Roseme orgasmed, the terrorist was gasping for breath, he got completely covered with Roseme's output, he yelled, "It smells like hell and vomited in Roseme's skirt!"

Roseme grabbed the terrorist by ear and said, "How the hell are you going to have sex with 72 virgins when you cannot even last for more than 2 minutes!"

Terrorist pleaded with folded hand and said, "Please forgive me sister, I have learned my lesson, now let me go, I will cut the head of the Maulavi who brainwashed me and send me to USA to kill Kafirs, in return, my Maulavi promised 72 virgins in heaven, I cannot even handle one virgin!"

Second terrorist came, I volunteered myself. The terrorist started to watch a porn clip in his smart phone and asked me to sit on his lap and massage his dick. I obliged and started moving my ass vigorously, I learned this move from famous Hollywood actress "Funny Leone". The terrorist asked me to stop, I did not, within 5 minutes, the terrorist ejaculated inside his pant. I was sexually excited, I asked the terrorist to wear condom and make love with me. The terrorist stared crying, "He said, he never thought, he would ejaculate within minutes, so far in porn movies, he saw guys having sex for hours, he was ready to make love with all 20 of us."

Unlike Roseme, I did not ask the terrorist to satisfy myself. I asked the terrorist, "What are you going to do with 72 virgin, if you cannot even satisfy a single girl?" The terrorist pleaded with folded hands, "Sister, you have opened my eyes, I was blindly believing the Maulavi in our mosque in Pakistan. Now I am convinced that 72 virgins is a fairy tale, we will never get them to make love with!"

I quipped, "Your penis will rot in grave, how are you going to make love with 72 virgins in heaven? Please go back to Pakistan and live happily, killing Kafirs and then getting killed by formidable American army is sheer stupidity!"

Third terrorist came, my friend borkha volunteered. The terrorist asked borkha to do a mini strip tease before making love.

Borkha started strip tease, which she learnt from famous Hollywood actress "Funny Leone". The terrorist started masturbating ogling at borkha's increasingly naked body. After two minutes, the terrorist made a loud sound out of pleasure, his pant was completely wet.

Borkha was completely frustrated, Roseme started laughing and said, "At least, I got what I wanted, you two were unlucky today! Better luck tomorrow."

Borkha slapped the terrorist mildly and said, "Are you convinced that you do not need 72 virgins? Go back to Pakistan and get married, if you can satisfy even .05% of her sexual needs, consider yourself a great man!"

The third terrorist did not have any answer. He left our "Free Sex" camp completely dejected.

Remaining two terrorists lost their way and in lieu of returning to our "Free Sex Camp", they entered a "Free Medical Camp" in Bermuda with erect dick and demanded sex. They were shot in their dicks and died on the spot. May almighty give them peace, may they be wiser in their next birth and may they do not believe in the false "fairy tale of 72 virgins to kill Kafirs".

We continued our "Free Sex Camp" for a month. The infiltration in our area become ZERO! "USA Army" took complete credit of bringing down the infiltration to zero. But it was our "Married but Available" sex camp, which helped terrorists to understand that, "They do not need 72 virgins, they cannot even handle one virgin". UN must recognize our patriotic contribution and award our "Married but Available" group "Nobel Peace Prize", otherwidr we will withdraw ourselves from the "Free Sex" camp and terrorism will return in United States Of America. On the other hand, if we get "Nobel Peace Prize", we will become famous in USA, many more "Married But Available" girls will join our group and we can run our "Free Sex Camp" till "so called" Pakistanis terrorists stop infiltrating USA. The fate of "ongoing Jihad against USA is now at the hand of UN now.

Let's make "Married But Available" great again. God Bless America. Now read the story of my 12th boyfriend who migrated from Australia to "Make America Great Again".

Prologue

It's November 1985 in Sydney, Australia. Two parents were at Doctor Orange's chamber with their child. Doctor Orange recommended liver test to the child. The child was diagnosed to have stage IV liver cancer, a rare type of childhood disease. Doctor Orange informed the parent, "Your baby's liver is severely damaged and there is only 4% chance that he would live!" The parents busted into tears. Doctor Orange patted the parents in back and said, "I would try my best to cure your son". The American doctor could indeed cure the child. That child was me and it was my parents. I had experienced American ingeniousness first hand in my life. In fact, it was only because of Dr. Orange's magic touch, I am alive today. I am also a bestselling author.

Had I not migrated to USA, I could have been just an ordinary pizza delivery guy in a remote Sydney Suburb.

I had a dream of migrating to America

From the early childhood, I had a strong desire to visit America. The first word I seemed to have spoken was "Orange", the capitalistic symbol of America. I used to often talk about America in my school, they thought, "John was a retard!" I would prove all my schoolmates and teachers wrong one day. My dad came from Kenya, mom came from Iraq. My mom was not at all inclined to take me to USA, she used to consider America a "Policed state with many ghettos". To discourage me from pursuing my American dream, she used to often show me news about shooting among gangs in Chicago, etc. My dad had a choice to either migrate to USA or Australia. I was sure, if he would have migrated to America in lieu of Australia, I would not had to suffer in this desert country.

My parents were anti American, I was raised to believe that America was the "big bad boy" of the world. My mom used to say, "America steals oil from Middle East and sells trillion dollar fake bonds to live a lavished life. America would never be able to repay back the 14+ trillion dollar debts!" None of this could extinguish my burning desire to settle down in America!

Then 9/11 happened, I was horrified to see large towers crashing down to ground and killing 3000 Americans. That very day, I decided to migrate to America at any cost. America needs to be rebuilt and protected from all evil forces of the world

December 2013, I applied for "immigration visa" to USA against my parent's will. Within a month, I was called for an Interview to "US Consulate". The consular official asked me to for a blowjob as a favor for approving my visa. I refused it immediately. He got very offended and said, "Now even God will not be able to send you to America!" He put my Visa in "Under Consulate Review" state forever. I was losing all hopes to migrate to USA. As luck would have it the interviewer died due to HIV. I thanked God for taking that perverted bastard above quickly, I could have easily contracted HIV from that sex starved bastard! Another person took over his position, he was young and diligent officer, I was asked to appear for another interview which I cleared with ease. It was December 2015, I finally got my visa to USA.

I immediately borrowed 10000 AUD from my Parent and flew to USA and landed in Houston. After standing 2 hours in the "immigration queue", I went to the immigration counter. The immigration counter official asked me to not smile while he was taking my photograph. The immigration officer handed down me a set of questions to test my knowledge about America. I answered them to my best ability. The immigration officer warned me not to use Google to search for answers. I attach the questions and answers at the end of this book. This would help all persons wanting to immigrate to USA legally.

The immigration officer was extremely pleased with my answers, he stood up and shook my hand and said, "You are a genius, 90% people coming to America fails this entrance test and they are vetted one more round!"

At the airport homeland security groped my body brutally and he was still not happy, he took me to a room and searched my cavities for drugs. I hated this very much but the joy of reaching USA was overwhelming my anger.

I took a cab to Kingwood. The driver was Chinese, surprisingly from my accent he could figure out that I was an Australian. He had worked in Australia before, he was fascinated about Australia. He had applied for permanent residency in Australia but it was not granted so he moved to Mexico and crossed the border to come to USA.

The cab driver asked, "Why the hell did you migrate from Australia to USA, in compared to USA, Australia is heaven, no Dindu problem, no police atrocity, low racism, etc."

I said, "I feel, America is more open than Australia. Unless you have got a God father, you cannot make much progress, Australia is country of gate keepers!"

The cab driver yelled, "You are going to get a shock of your life, you will repent the decision to migrate to America."

I said, "I am already enjoying USA, it's much better than Australia"

I got down from the cab, it was late evening, and cold breeze was blowing. I put down my leather jacket, I was still shivering. I would have to buy a new jacket soon.

Handling Dindus

While crossing a lane, a young dindu interrupted me and asked for cigarette, I did not have any, the dindu got offended and said, "Why have come to America? Go back to your Country!"

I got irritated and said, "Why do not you go back to your Country?"

The dindu got infuriated and took out a small knife and tried to stab me, I was much stronger than the young dindu, I moved to my left, the dindu missed striking me, I caught his right hand and twisted it so hard, and the small knife fall down on the drain.

I left the dindu and asked him to get lost. He searched for his knife, he could not get it, the dindu saw a police van passing by, he yelled at the police van asking it to stop. Two armored policemen came and asked the dindu, "What's the matter?"

The dindu started crying and said, "This white man called me a nigger and he twisted my hand very hard, he stole 100 USD from me!" The dindu then yelled something in his dindu language, five more dindus came from nowhere, with posters reading "Dindu Lives Matter! We will fight for equal rights till the end!" One fat dindu woman put a bandage on the hand of that young dindu. They demanded that I be arrested and put in jail for hurling racist abuse and hurting a young dindu.

To my great surprise, I discovered that one of the police was also a dindu, he started talking with the dindu group, in dindu language. The other policeman interrupted and said, "Let's hear from the other gentleman."

He asked, "Why did you abuse and beat a dindu, it's an unpardonable crime!"

I said, "Young dindu tried to stab me, hence I had to twist his hand

The young dindu yelled, "Do not believe this white man, where is the knife?"

The knife had fallen in the drain, I took the police near the drain and pointed to the spot where knife was dropped. There was no knife at that spot. The police said, "Shut up, you are lying! You beat an innocent dindu, now you will be charged with hate crime!" The police handcuffed me and took me to Texas Jail. I met many ugly people inside Texas jail.

Only one religion is true

I met famous Muslim preacher "Zakir Nalayak" who had converted thousands non-believers to Islam, whose videos allegedly inspired people to become terrorists and get 72 virgins in heaven quickly.

I: Zakir brother, I am your big fan, I got few questions about Islam, will you be able you answer them?

Zakir: Sure Johnuddin.

I: I am John not Johnuddin, my first question is, Verse 9:29 of Quran states following:

Fight those who do not believe in Allah or in the Last Day and who do not consider unlawful what Allah and His Messenger have made unlawful and who do not

adopt the religion of truth from those who were given

the Scripture - [fight] until they give the jizyah willingly

while they are humbled.

So my question is, Allah has mandated all Muslims to fight non-believers till they convert or pay hefty tax, do not you think, this is inhuman?

Zakir: Brother Johnuddin has asked a very good question, that Allah asked Muslims to kill non-believers, but brother, you must know the context of the verse, those apparent violent verses are applicable only when Muslims are at war with non-believers.

I: Then ISIS has declared war against non-believers and raping/killing/enslaving non-believers exactly as mentioned in Quran.

Zakir: No you are wrong, ISIS is also killing Muslims

I: Yes, they are killing those Muslims who do not follow Quran 100% like Sufi Muslims, etc.

Zakir: You are wrong Johnuddin, chapter 5, page 20, line number 2, even your God asked people to kill their enemies, right?

I: Assume only Quran is 100% true and rest all religions are mythology, do you agree that Quran has violent verses and millions of Muslims are misinterpreting those verses and treating non-believers inhumanly, due to misinterpretation of Quran, millions of non-believers are losing their lives. Thousands of non-believers are taken as sex slave by ISIS. How does Allah permit that?

Zakir: It is allowed by Allah, I cannot question it.

I: Why do not you remove all violent verses for Quran and publish a modern peaceful Quran? Why are you giving Jihadi Muslims a chance to misinterpret Quran and kill/rape/enslave non-believers, for the sake of humanity, publish a modern peaceful Quran and ensure that all Muslims follow modern Quran?

Zakir: Quran is God's word, not an alphabet can be changed, there will be riots across world, and we will behead all those who say, "Islam is violent"

I: But USA, Russia, Israel may retaliate and annihilate Saudi Arabia

Zakir: Then I will join the fight against non-believers, I would not mind dying fighting holy Jihad, in heaven I would be granted 72 virgins, I can have fun with them eternally

I: But Zakir brother, your penis will be rotting in your grave, what you will do with 72 virgins in heaven?

Zakir: Do not question my religion, Allah is one and only God!

I: That's just your belief, science does not believe in God

Zakir ran toward me and grabbed my throat and said: You fucking infidel, you will burn in hell forever, convert to Islam else I will kill you now.

I: Leave my throat, I will accept Islam.

Zakir: That's like a good boy, I will get you circumcised tonight, Dr. Kana Gayyub is my good friend, and she has performed hundreds of conversion surgery.

You would enjoy losing the skin in the soft hand of Dr. Kana Gayyub. I will get some beef by bribing the Jailor, that's it, from now on, you must say "Allah Ho Akbar" at every possible opportunity and pray to Allah 5 times per day, your new name will be Johnuddin. Suddenly Police came from nowhere and snatched myself away for Zakir's hand. Zakir tried to snatch myself back from Police. Zakir yelled at police and said, "You infidels cannot prevent me from preaching Islam!" Police tased Dr. Zakir and he fall down on ground, he hurled some abuse to the police in Arabic.

Please keep gays in different cell of Jail

I met few GayActivists in Texas jail, my experience with them was horrible, they took my virginity, I had just spent 3 days in Texas Jail, on 4th midnight, I felt, someone had climbed on top of me, and I was lying naked, and one brute was banging my ass, I felt someone has inserted a knife in my ass, blood started coming out, I could turn around and hit him in throat, but other GayActivists were waiting for their turn with their pants down, they grabbed me, tied me to the jail bars and raped me for almost 2 hours. I never failed so shameful in my life, I thought, "How will show my face in my village, once they come to know that, I was gang raped by GayActivists in Texas Jail.

They said, they enjoyed it so much that they would do this every night, till I get bail, now I understand why many jail comit suicide in Texas jail. I thought of committing suicide than tolerating rape, in my suicide note I wrote, "Hail Uncle Sam, Gay sex should be banned in all American jails, I cannot take it any more". Uncle Sam came in my dreams and asked me to meet "Burnie Sanders" for a solution to the GayActivists problem. In the next morning, I went to meet "Burnie Sanders", I shook his hand and told him about my plight.

Burnie Sanders: Oh boy, just do not wash your ass properly after shitting

I stopped washing ass after shitting, next night the gay gang tried same trick, first guy who tried to rape me had his dick full of shits, he started vomiting, other GayActivists decided to dump me and try another immigrant.

Police presented me to court, the judge asked to share video recording of that lane for that period so that my crime could be proved beyond any doubt. On next hearing, judge watched the video and yelled at those two police who had arrested me for racial crime, "Why the hell could not you watch the video before putting this innocent man in Jail?"

The dindu police said, "A large dindu group gathered to protest, if we would not have arrested this gentleman from the spot, the dindu groups could have damaged our police van, they could have even killed us!"

The judge said to me, "I am sorry Gentleman, you are free to leave."

I lost all the money I had. I was forced to work in a car wash for 12 hours per day for a month.

Car washing was draining my physical energy, I was just sleeping, waking up, going to "Car Wash

Company" and eating in the KFCs. I was missing "Great Australian Life" a lot.

I then got an interview call from "Taj Finance", there were four rounds of interview and after the interview. They offered me a job and asked me to come to office on next Monday. I was extremely happy, I resigned from my car wash company, the owner of the carwash gave me a hug and paid me my dues and said, "My door will remain open for you always!" I updated my LinkedIn profile with job title "Computer Admin at Taj Finance".

I arrived at "Taj Finance" office on Monday at 8 am sharply. There was an induction program at 8:30 am, A beautiful company secretary took my documents and made me sign few papers. As the induction progressed, I understood that this job is not computer related, it was just a salesperson job. I would have to beg people to donate 30 USD for helping cancer victim. Out of 30 USD I would get 30% commission, company would take 60% of the money as admin fee and remaining 10% USD would be spent for cancer victims. I yelled, "What about Salary?" The smart trainer retorted, "We do not restrict your income as Salary, if you get 1000 people to sign up for cancer fund, you will get 9000 USD!"

This hurt my Australian pride badly, I would not be able to stand in road and talk to unknown arrogant Americans and make them sign up for donating to cancer victim. I could not sleep that night. I was supposed to stand near Houston airport next morning. Next morning I called the person whom I was supposed to report at Houston airport and said, "I am sorry, I would not come to work!" The officer yelled at me, "You have signed a legal agreement with our company, you have to work at least 4 weeks! Otherwise we will send you legal notice." My Australian pride aroused and I yelled, "You fucking bastard advertise a salesman job as computer admin and then refuse to pay salary and just donate 10% of the amount to cancer victim! Go and sue me, your company will get busted in no time." The officer cut my call.

Falling in Love in USA

By Uncle Sam's blessing, I fall in love with Dr. Kana Gayyub, the awesome doctor whom I heard about at Texas Jail. She had come to my room to take my interview. It was early morning. She was wearing a sleeveless blue top and pink mini skirt.

Kana said, "Hi John, I got your contact from my teacher Dr. Zakir Nalayak. I would like to interview you and publish it in my upcoming book "Deprived Dindus". I smiled at her and started ogling at her as if I never saw any girl before, I said, "Let's close the door, government has deployed lot of spies to disrupt our freedom movement"

Kana showed interest in me by repeatedly putting her arms above her head to let me inspect her shaved armpit and overflowing breast. She was enjoying my unfailing attention.

I was thinking of tying her in the bed and force her to enact my favorite porn videos. Kana got slightly scared, she folded her legs and started the interview.

Kana Gayyub: My objective for this interview is to show white Americans in poor light, so that we can convert black Americans to Islam and once we became majority, we will make America as great as Syria, Somalia, Kenya, etc.

I thought, "Is Kana color blind to consider me non-white, I thought of telling her the truth but I could have done anything for the jasmine perfume emanating from her freshly bathed body."

I said, "Kana, we have so much in common, you are Kana, I am John, our name rhymes well, your skirt's color is red, which is my favorite color, red is the color of Love."

Ms. Kana said, "Come on Mr. John, do not flirt with me like that."

Ms. Kana thought, "This bastard is trying to impress me, but I am not here to date him, I am here to gather material for one chapter of my upcoming book 'Deprived Dindus', hope John does not pounce upon me before I finish the interview, if he does, I will bite him in the neck and teach him a lesson of his life, he is ogling at me like a perverted bastard. Let me give him some hint that I am not interested to get laid!"

Ms. Kana said, "You are funny person, my skirt is Pink not red!"

I thought, "Once I take it out, color would not matter!"

Kana: Have you ever been denied job due to your skin color?

John: Many times, I still do not have a permanent job, even though I am highly qualified, I am forced to work on menial jobs like carwash, etc.

Ms. Kana: Do you consider that as color based discrimination?

I: Sure.

Kana: All non-white American must convert to Islam, we do not believe in color, creed, sect, etc. Our religion preaches "Universal Brotherhood" and peace.

I thought, "I would not be able to control my passions for long" and said, "You are genius Ms. Kana, can I give you a hug?"

Kana thought, "If I allow John a hug so early, I would be lying in his bed within an hour and my interview would not be completed, I would not be able to finish my book 'Deprived Dindus' on time. I have already taken 10000 USD advance from publisher!"

Kana: You are a funny man, let's complete the interview first.

I thought, "I am going grab Ms. Kana and kiss her everywhere. I cannot control my passion till the end of Interview, hope Kana does not file a rape case on me, I would not want to go back to Texas jail under any circumstance, rape convicts are treated worse than animals by 'Gay Activists' in Texas Jail."

I said, "Kana, Have you got a boyfriend?"

Kana said with a smile, "No, I just broke up with my sixth live in partner recently, let's complete the interview first, we can talk about other things later!"

I said, "I am longing for love for a long time."

Kana thought, "This bastard is wasting my time, let me quickly ask my questions and get out of here, else I will surely be raped by John!"

Kana said, "Mr. John, It's almost 15 minutes, I could ask you only one question, if it continues like that, I will have to stay with you still mid night, you may be losing many opportunities, let's complete the interview quickly."

I thought, "I will not mind staying with you forever, I just need to take off your cloth and lie on top of your naked body forever."

Kana asked: "Have you ever been denied service by white American?"

I said, "Many times! I neither had drinking water nor money to buy mineral water bottles. Many white shop owners used to shoe me away.

Kana sobbed, "That's unimaginable!"

I moved closer to Kana and tapped her on the back and said, "Do not worry, we will liberate America from white aggression, we will build an America free from all kind of deprivation."

I started rubbing my knee against Kana's mini skirt, Kana allowed it for a minute and got scared and moved away little bit.

I said, "Ms. Kana, you are looking awesome, can I give you hug please?"

Kana said, "Sure."

I grabbed her like a bear, smelled her jasmine scent. I looked at her eyes, lips, face, arms very closely.

Kana started breathing heavily. She closed her eyes, I started kissing her lip, cheek, and throat. Her breasts were getting pressed against my chest.

Ms. Kana yelled, "You got what you wanted, now let me go please!"

I released her from my bear hug and dragged her to my smelly bed, there was smell of masturbation everywhere, I was apprehensive that foul smell would offend Kana and kill my chance to make love with her.

I said with lot of expectation, "Kana, I love you very much, sweet heart!"

Kana said, "See John, we can date some other day, let me go, I need to complete my book 'Deprived Dindus' by next week, after that I would be free!"

I started rubbing Kana's leg using my knee, the masturbation smell seemed to have aroused Ms. Kana slightly. She allowed me to continue massaging her legs.

Kana yelled, "Listen Mr. John, I have got very low sex drive, I am ready to let you hug, kiss and massage me. I would not let you make love, it hurts me badly!"

I accepted the challenge and said, "Ms. Kana, if I cannot arouse you sexually, I would let you go"

I made her sit on my Lap. I started showing her my porn video collections one by one. Kana was still pretty unemotional. I cupped her breasts and massaged them gently, she seemed to enjoy it. After sometime she said, "See John, I am not at all interested in sex, if you force sex on me, it would amount to rape, let me go please, I need to complete my book 'Deprived Dindus' by next week!"

I was getting frustrated with her, even after groping, kissing, hugging and massaging her for an hour, she was still not allowing me to have sex. In the porn videos, girl start moaning from the moment, guys touch her. It feels so good to even masturbate watching porn videos. But this bitch, even after one hour of foreplay and watching porn videos, was still not allowing me to make love."

My hands was paining, I should had let Ms. Kana go. I should have just masturbated watching porn videos to settle for the day.

I asked her frustratingly, "Tell me Ms. Kana, what makes you horny?"

Ms. Kana said, "Reading Dora Robert's novels, when I feel very lonely, I read her novels and satisfy myself thinking about scenes depicted in the novel!"

I jumped on my feet, even I was a big fan of "Dora Robert". I had read Dora Robert's novels many times, but it had never aroused me sexually. I took out 5 Dora Robert's novel from shelf, "Island of Gays", "Stars of Misfortune", "From This Night", "Heaven and Hell",

"Tears of the Sun" and "Dance Upon The Air" and asked her to read them one by one.

Kana yelled, "You idiot, do you think, I will sit on your lap whole day and read Dora Robert's books?"

I said, "Please explain, I am unable to understand your girly tricks."

Kana said, "Ok, just read page 57 of 'From This Night' yourself and do exactly what is written there!"

Kana lied down on my smelly bed with lot of anticipation.

She stretched her leg slightly. I read page 57 of "From This Night". As mentioned in the novel, I took out her miniskirt, took out her pantie. I started rubbing her inner thigh, inner curve, etc. I said, "Your body is softer than butter!"

The book read, "Once you rub the girl's inner curve and praise them verbally, the girl will get very wet, then you can do whatever you want with her."

But Ms. Kana was still very dry! I got stuck in next line of page 57, "It asked me to use my mouth and tongue into a place which is filled with germs, pus, blood and sweat!" It gave me a "Yuck" feeling, I again thought of letting Ms. Kana go. Kana yelled, "Do exactly what is mentioned in the book quickly, else I will dress up and leave you forever!" I obliged, I was like a pig who could do anything for sex, I used my mouth to bite her private part softly, used my tongue to lick it, finally Ms. Kana started getting wet. The smell emanating from Ms. Kana was much worse than rotten milk! I went to Bathroom to vomit.

Once I came back from bathroom, "Ms. Kana was rubbing her private part and moaning softly, she was breathing heavily."

Ms. Kana said, "I am ready for love but you have to satisfy me completely." I took out my pant and shirt, took her top out. I was unable to open her bra, so I tore it off. My dream of having real sex with a real girl was finally coming true. But luck never favored myself, as I was suffering from slight EDS problem, whenever I used to wear condom, I used to lose erection, but I could not afford to make Ms. Kana pregnant from our 'One Day Stand', I took out a condom and started wearing it, hoping that Uncle Sam will cure my EDS temporarily. The moment I wore condom, my 6 inch erect dick became a 3 inch sphere, I yelled at myself out of frustration, "Shame on you John, a naked girl lying on bed is wet and aroused and your bastard dick betrayed you at the right moment, oh 'Uncle Sam', please help me now!"

Kana moaned in soft voice, "Please do not use condom, it's a sin to use condom!" That single sentence aroused my dick again, I threw off the condom in the dustbin. I pounced upon her as if I was a tiger and she was my deer. I went inside her, she started moaning like my favorite porn star. I was squeezing her boobs, kissing her madly.

She repeatedly asked me, "Do you love me John? Will you marry me? How many kids shall we have?"

I repeatedly said, "I love you sweetheart, I will definitely marry you, we will make two kids, one boy and one girl"

I was inside her for two minutes, I was about to come, so I tried to pull it out of her, she grabbed me like a python and did not allow me pull out and said,

"It's a sin to waste DNA, it feels so good inside. Do not you want me to enjoy your DNA?"

I thought, "If I put my DNA into her and she becomes pregnant, from where I will pay child support? I will let Ms. Kana give the child for adoption, John's DNA can easily become next 'Steve Jobs', etc."

I put all my DNA inside her, it felt so well. I prayed to Uncle Sam, "For God's sake, please do not make her pregnant!"

I said, "Ms. Kana, I am ready to marry you, I have never enjoyed so much in my life. Every day I used to masturbate watching porn videos, but sex with you felt 10 times better, I cannot live without you."

Kana said, "Are you willing to convert to Islam?"

I said, "See, I am a liberal, liberals do not believe in God, so If I convert to Islam, I will become a laughing stock. Converting to Islam would end my political aspiration, hence it is not possible for me to convert to any religion. But I will not force you to convert to liberalism, it's a deal!"

I said, "Let me tell you a truth, I am actually white, because I worked in a car wash company for few weeks, you can see few black spots on my skin"

Kana said, "You white bastard, you had consensual sex with me by hiding your color, I would file a rape case against you for hiding your color"

I said, "Color, creed, religion does not matter for me, why do not become more open minded, not all upper class people are bad. I tried my best to pleasure you."

Kana said, "I do not want any white bastard, give me 5000 USD immediately else I will shout rape and get you arrested right now"

I said, "Relax sweet heart, we will come up with a solution in cool head!"

Kana said, "I enjoyed sex for the first time in my life, my ex live in partner used to force sex on me, he used to hurt me badly, I could not tolerate it for long. I kicked him in his balls. He packed all my luggage and put it in road and asked me to vacate his apartment immediately."

I said, "I will never leave you, we will live a happily married life forever!"

Ms. Kana said, "If you do not convert to Islam, my family will not accept you as son in law, they will hire a hit man to get you killed. Please convert for my sake, I will satisfy all your sexual desires."

I thought, "If I refuse to convert, I have to pay her 5000 USD for sex, that's too costly for a lady who already had six sex partners! "

I said, "Kana Darling, please give me two weeks' time, I will decide whether I can convert to Islam or not!"

I thought, "After two weeks, the bitch would not be able to prove rape charge against me, her priority may change completely. Worst case, I would be slapped with a cheating case, I will bribe the judge and get that case squashed."

Kana said, "Ok, give me a hug and kiss, I gave you everything, if you betray me now, even 'Uncle Sam' will not forgive you!"

Kana used my mirror to put lipsticks, straighten her hair. After a stormy sex session, she was looking like disheveled bird after a storm. Both I and Ms. Kana was completely exhausted from sex. She went to bathroom, she took bath, dressed herself. I again hugged her like a bear and cupped her breasts, when she came to my hostel room, she was looking like a dry tree waiting for rain. After getting my DNA, she was looking like a fully blossomed tree.

I gifted Dora Robert's "From This Night" to Ms. Kana Gayyub to immortalize our "love story".

Two weeks passed by. Ms. Kana called me and said, "Ok, I am going to meet you tonight at your room, by that time, you must decide whether you are ready to convert, otherwise I would have to find someone else!"

I started in waiting in anticipation of another steamy sex session with Ms. Kana tonight. I bought a gas mask to ensure that "spoiled milk" smell does not make me vomit again.

Ms. Kana arrived in my room by 9 PM, I opened the window of my room to let fresh air come inside. This time, Kana bought another person with him, the renowned preacher Dr. Zakir Nalayak. I felt scared and betrayed.

Zakir said, "As-Salaam-Alaikum, Mr. Johnuddin"

I said, "As-Salaam-Alaikum Zakir Brother, when were you released from Tihar jail? By the way, you forgot my name again, I am John not Johnuddin!"

Zakir said, "Funny thing happened brother Khanuddin, I could brain wash the atheist judge who was hearing my bail plea, he converted to Islam and then convincing him was like a piece of cake walk, since the Judge had to abide by Sharia now, he had no choice other than releasing me on Bail."

Zakir continued, "If you convert to Islam tonight, we would be able to convert thousands of immigrants in a month's time, every month, our follower will double. In 10 years, we will establish 'Islamic State of USA, Inshallah."

I said, "I am a Liberal, I do not believe in any Allah/God/Jesus."

Ms. Kana yelled, "You betrayed me, you took my virginity and now you are refusing to marry me!" Tears were rolling down from the soft cheek of Ms. Kana.

I said, "Wait, you had 6 sex partners before me, how are you claiming yourself to be virgin?"

Ms. Kana said, "Well, you are the first person, who helped me reach orgasm, I really want to marry you, we will make love every day, please convert for my sake. It's very easy, Dr. Zakir will let you recite Holy verses and then you will eat roasted beef and I will circumcise you with utmost care, your name would be slightly changed to Johnuddin, that's it, tomorrow we will go to a Qazi and get married ."

I said, "Forced conversation is Illegal, you cannot blackmail people to convert to your religion!"

Dr. Zakir said, "Brother Johnuddin, you do not have much options left, convert to Islam and marry Ms. Kana or else we will file a rape case against you. You will languish in Texas jail for lifetime. Did you forget what the 'Gay Activists' do to you last time?"

I asked Dr. Zakir to get out of my room for few minutes so that I could discuss few private things with Ms. Kana.

Dr. Zakir went outside my room, he put his ear on the door of my room.

I grabbed Ms. Kana and forced her to sit on my Lap and said in a low voice, "Honey, why do we have to marry? We can live in like this as long we like each other. Once we get bored, you find someone from your religion."

Ms. Kana was getting aroused, she was moving her body gently and breathing heavily. She said, "You must convert to Islam tonight, I do not want to lose you, I want to marry you and get settled, I am fed up with living in with liberal bastards who just want my body, I want someone like you, who will love me with body, mind and soul!"

I said, "Ok, I will recite Holy verses and eat roasted beef, but I will not change my name to Johnuddin nor will I circumcise, is that a deal?"

Ms. Kana started sobbing loudly, "You bastard, you took everything from me. But you are not willing to convert. I will commit suicide and put your name in my suicide note."

Dr. Zakir Nalayak came running inside and threatened me, "Mr. Johnuddin, if Ms. Kana commits suicide, Inshallah, I will send my students to Australia to behead all your family members."

Ms. Kana was still sitting on my lap, she felt very awkward and stood up.

I said, "Ok, I will not convert, I will pay blood money of 5000 USD, just give me a month to arrange for the money! For God's sake, please do not file any rape case, whatever happened between us was absolutely consensual, Ms. Kana herself confessed that she could orgasm for the first time in her life!"

Ms. Kana and Dr. Zakir Nalayak left for the day, they lost the opportunity to convert me.

I begged in front of Houston airport to collect Ms. Kana's blood money.

On 30th day, I could finally collect 5000 USD as donation, I went to meet Ms. Kana. I threw 5000 USD on her face and said, "Bitch, you enjoyed the orgasm but still I had to beg in street for a month to pay you 5000 USD as blood money, now take it and fuck off from my life!" Ms. Kana collected the cash from ground and left the place sobbing. I was not sure why the hell was she crying. She got 5000 USD and an orgasm from me for free.

Making Trump Great Again

Following extreme harassment at the hand of dindus, I resolved to defeat OSAMA (The great master of dindus) in upcoming election at November 2017. I was a great artist, I drew few Trump pictures and started distributing free copies in public places. I told them, "It has been scientifically proven that, Coloring "Trump pictures" reduces anxiety, stress, etc." I ended up distributing 10000 of "Trump Coloring Pages" for free. Total cost of the whole exercise was more than 10k USD.

This was a Psychological warfare on the sheep population of USA, whoever took "Trump coloring pages" from me, they would have surely voted for Trump. Since coloring Trump would create a favorable impression of Trump in their stupid mind. Thanks to my coloring book Idea, trump won all seats in Texas. My hard work finally paid off.

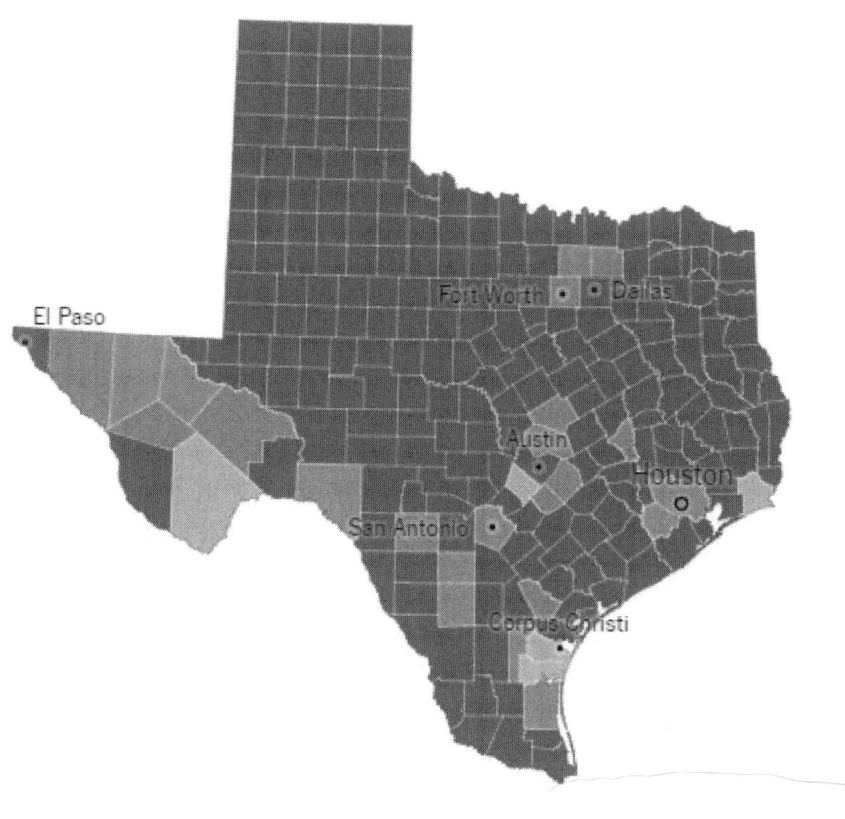

Making Immigration Great Again

Here are my eleven point ideas to deal with legal and illegal immigrants in America:

1. Cancel all existing work permits, H1-B visas, let companies hire local students, unemployed persons

2. Most of the Americans feel ashamed to take up job of toilet cleaning, road cleaning, plumbing, temporary maids, farming, etc. USA must issue work permit to all Illegal

Mexicans/Chinese/Indian working on such professions

3. Income tax for all non-Americans working in USA must be raised to 60%

4. Any American who asks another American to go back to his country should be deported to his original country

5. If American workers could not replace a percentage of H1-B, just auction all H1-B visas to highest bidder

6. Do not go for "Point based Immigration" like Canada, Australia. I have observed many highly qualified Chinese, Indians, Mexicans are forced to work in routine jobs(e.g. cleaning toilet, cleaning road, etc.) after coming to Australia

7. Divert 1% of defense budget to bring mosques, dindu joints, etc. under advanced surveillance

8. Take "American Entrance Test" at the country of boarding itself, this way, cost of coming to USA and getting deported from USA would be saved

9. Remove all violent verses from Quran and publish a modern Quran, force all mosques, Muslim preachers to use the modern Quran to conduct Islam

10.   Deport all immigrants currently languishing in jail. It's a sheer wastage of tax payer's money to feed people who should not have been to USA at the first place.

11. Deport all citizens with violent crime record to their original country, take help of DNA test to confirm ancestry, in case ancestry could not be determined. By default deport him/her to Africa. Since human civilization started from Africa. Africa must take care of the people who stopped evolving and are a threat to America.

Thanks for reading. Hail Trump. Make America Great Again.

American Entrance Test

Question: Name few things that grows in America

Answer: National Debt, Crime Rate, Politician's Bank Balance, Corporate profit.

Question: Why does American girl insists not to have more than three Children?

Answer: Because, every fourth children born in World is a Chinese and Americans hate them

Question: Why do American go to movie in a group of 18 or more?

Answer: Because, Under 17 group is not allowed to enter.

Question: How will you prove that toothbrush was indeed invented in America?

Answer: Otherwise it would have been called teethbrush.

Question: How to break a USA graduate finger?

Answer: Punch him in nose.

Question: What is the main difference between a bowling ball and American Girl?

Answer: Bowling ball is more difficult to pick up.

Question: What do American graduates use for birth control

Answer: Withdrawal at the last moment.

Question: What is the main difference between America and Yogurt?

Answer: Yogurt has living culture.

Question: Why did an American Dindu cross the road?

Answer: Because he was released from jail.

Question: How to make an American Blonde laugh in weekend?

Answer: Tell her a joke on Monday.

Question: Why was not Jesus born in America?

Answer: A virgin of conceivable age could not be found.

Question: What's most used book in "University of Texas"?

Answer: Coloring Book.

Question: Why are there many unsolved murder in Texas?

Answer: There are no dental records and everyone has similar DNA.

Question: Why was thirty students of "University of Texas" struck on escalator for 3 hours?

Answer: There was three hours of power cut at Texas.

Question: Why did America disband its water polo team?

Answer: Horses could not swim and drown in the water.

Question: What's the difference between an American diploma and toilet paper?

Answer: 50000 USD per page.

Question: How do you confuse an American?

Answer: You cannot do that, they are born that way.

Question: What is the Texas state slogan?

Answer: Oils wells that ends well.

Question: What is the definition of safe sex in America?

Answer: Placing signs on animals that kick.

Question: What's full form of TGIF?

Answer: Toes Go In First.

Question: What should you do if you find three American buried till neck in cement?

Answer: Get more cements.

Question: Why are rectal thermometers banned in USA?

Answer: They cause too much brain damage.

Question: How did the American die while drinking milk?

Answer: The cow slipped on the spilled milk and fall on him.

Question: What does an American and beer bottle in common?

Answer: They are both empty from the neck up.

Question: What's the first thing an American girl do after waking up in the morning?

Answer: She goes to home.

Question: What's favorite whine for Americans?

Answer: We cannot beat Canadians.

Question: What do you call an American football player with championship ring?

Answer: A thief.

Question: How do you prevent an American from beating his wife?

Answer: Dress her like a Canadian.

Question: What's the difference between a bucket of shit and an American?

Answer: The bucket.

Question: What is the only country in world, where you can get a divorce but still be brother and sister?

Answer: United States of America.

Question: Why don't girls play hide and seek in Texas?

Answer: None would look for them.

Question: How do you separate the men from boys in America?

Answer: Give them free condoms, whoever does not accept is a boy.

Question: How to keep Mexicans out of America

Answer: Deport all Mexicans and build a wall and make Mexico pay for it

I thank http://Jokes4US.com/ for helping me prepare well for "American Entrance Test".

About Author

Pamela Lewinsky is dashing brilliant generation X "thought leader" from USA. Her idea, "Terrorism did not kill my uncle, USA Pakistan war did" was heavily appreciated across many nations like Syria, Somalia, Pakistan and India. USA media calls her, "The Mallala Yousuf" of America. Pamela hopes to get noble prize in peace for coming up with a practical solution to end terrorism from world once and for all.

If you are planning to make a movie/TV serial out of this bestselling book, please contact johntrumpet_@outlook.com

Printed in Great Britain
by Amazon